MYLES

JUMP the LINE

How to Change Your Life and DNA Supernaturally!

Foreword: Apostle Lee Roberson

i

Published by

Francis Myles International (in partnership with)
Francis Myles Enterprises LLC
P.O. Box 2467
Scottsdale, Arizona, 85252

For Worldwide Distribution
Printed in the United States

Hall of Appreciation

"The Lord gave the word: great was the company of those that published it" (Psalm 68:11 KJV).

It has been said that great projects are never the work of one man, but the collective effort of a team that shares a common destiny. I want to give a heartfelt "God bless you" to the following brothers and sisters for making the publishing of this book a reality. May God give you a tremendous harvest for every person who will be transformed by the truths contained within.

My parents, Daniel and Ester Mbepa, for raising me in the fear of the Lord

My spiritual parents Dr. Ralph and Eileen Wilkerson, for your valuable spiritual covering

Dr. Gershom Sikaala for being such a dear friend and true prophet of God

Sid Roth and Its Supernatural Television Show for giving me the opportunity to bring this life changing revelation to the masses

Carmela Real Myles for being the love of my life and an amazing glue and connector for God's Kingdom

Apostle Lee and Prophetess April Roberson, for running with the jump the line message and bringing hope to many

Alumni of the Order of Melchizedek Supernatural School of Ministry

Members of Royal Priesthood International Embassy, for their passion for the Jump the Line message.

Foreword

As a Pastor you are always seeking for advantages, teachings, and technologies that would bring your followers great victory in their lives. When I received this revelation from Apostle Francis Myles this is exactly what I was looking for. It is the answer to many many questions that I personally had and many of our members. Several have testified during the same night of jumping into a new bloodline that cancer, stroke, suicide, back pain, and high blood pressure were all destroyed, and many more miracles, signs and wonders took place. My wife and I have traveled throughout America, many cities, many different states that have witnessed miracle after miracle as the same technology was presented. This technology takes you back to the origin, it changes the lives of people right before your eyes. We were not strangers to deliverance but we have never witnessed mass deliverance of this magnitude. This teaching from Breaking Generational Curses under the Order of Melchizedek will allow you to witness your family, your friends, and your peers receive the deliverance that they have been desperately seeking. I am grateful that we were in position to recrive this teaching and witness many lives change. I highly recommend this book for all Pastors, as well as all leaders. It will truly bring you the freedom that you seek and freedom for your followers and not only for your followers but the DNA of your house will witness a tremendous change.

Blessings on you,

Apostle Lee and Prophetess April Roberson
Sons of God Embassy
Kingsland, Georgia

PREFACE

On April 27, 1994 I was in the rainbow nation of South Africa. This rainbow nation on the southern coast of Africa is famous for its bloody history inspired by years of racially motivated apartheid. Generations of systemic racial degradation of the natives (mostly black people) by the white minority class had taken its toil on the soul and conscience of the fledgling nation. The lines of racial hatred and mistrust between whites and blacks were unmistakably visible; for a while it looked like this rainbow nation would never find the moral courage to cross the "LINE" that years of apartheid and bloodshed had forged in the soul of the nation.

The imprisonment of the late-great Nelson Mandela for twenty-seven years on the infamous Robben Island prison (South Africa's version of the infamous American prison, Alcatraz) only served to inflame even further the deep-seated feelings of hatred between whites and blacks. For many years it seemed as though Nelson Mandela and other civil rights leaders who were imprisoned with him would die in prison before the cancer of apartheid loosed its terrible grip on the troubled nation. But winds of change began to blow profusely when the outcry against apartheid from civilized nations grew louder. At the same time divine providence saw to it that a sympathetic, God-fearing white Christian President; Mr. De Klerk took the reigns of political power in South Africa in a landslide electoral victory.

Suddenly the impossible looked quite plausible as a racially divided country began to move towards crossing a "LINE" that had eluded the nation for centuries; the abolishment of the apartheid system of government. So, on April 27, 1994, South Africans held their first truly democratic elections, in which blacks and other minorities were allowed to participate as equal citizens. I experienced firsthand the glorious birth of a rainbow nation. The mood in the nation was a breathtaking mixture of somberness, fear and unfettered excitement as millions of South Africans stood in long, winding lines for hours, braving both the hot African Sun and torrential rains at polling stations for a once in a lifetime opportunity…**a dream come true!**

Nevertheless, the dream was so fragile; that many feared the dream would not survive the night…! They stood anxiously in long lines, fathers, mothers, sons, daughters, old and young to cast their first vote for the first black presidential candidate in a country that had been ravaged by an apartheid system that pitied its own citizenry in bloody wars based upon the color of their skin. I know of many white South Africans who actually voted for Mr. Nelson Mandela.

When Nelson Mandela was sworn in as South Africa's first black president on the 10th of May 1994, one billion people from around the world were glued to their TV sets, flanked by millions of teary eyed white and black South Africans who were just coming to terms with the fact that a **line** they never expected to be broken or crossed in their lifetime had just been shattered. **Shattered into a million pieces...and years later, a united rainbow nation continues to show that it was the right thing to do!**

However the most difficult lines to break or cross in life are **"blood lines."** These are lines that connect us in the bloodstream to people we know and many others we have never met. This book is a **roadmap** for how to achieve total victory over two classes of "LINES;" namely, **bloodlines and sidelines.** The main difference between these two classes of "LINES" will be explained within the pages of this book, so just keep reading till you get to the final chapter.

This book truly contains a divinely inspired method for overturning centuries of generational iniquity and demonically engineered genetic proclivities that are making it difficult for most Christians to live their life like Jesus did. It contains the **spiritual recipe of how you and I can change our life and DNA supernaturally!** What I write in this book was a direct revelation from a life changing spiritual encounter I had with the Lord Jesus Christ. I have dedicated a whole chapter to explain....how and where this encounter took place.

Yours for Kingdom Advancement

Dr. Francis Myles
Senior Pastor: Royal Priesthood International Embassy
Developer: Jump The Line Mobile App
Bestselling Author: The Order of Melchizedek
Copyright 2015

– JUMP the LINE –
Change your NOW!

Are there "lines" in life that YOU CAN'T SEEM TO CROSS?

What if there was one simple action YOU could take that would CHANGE EVERYTHING?

WOULD YOU DO IT?

CHAPTER ONE

LIFE IS FULL OF LINES

Life is all about lines. Life is so full of lines that even our roads are marked and governed by them. Our highways would be the most dangerous places to be if there were no lines on the tarmac to direct the flow of incoming and outgoing traffic. Most importantly, we all deal with lines in our private life, don't we?

- Lines between sadness and happiness

- Lines between loneliness and togetherness

- Lines between poverty and prosperity

- Lines between confusion and clarity

- Lines between hatred and forgiveness

- Lines between lust and love

And, lines between bondage and freedom!

Interestingly, it seems like **invisible lines** usually govern the areas of life most often labeled **impossible**. These invisible lines are lines we don't seem to see too clearly. For most of us, it's the lines between "impossible" and "possible" that are quite important and deeply personal for all of us. And, in most cases, doesn't it seem like that the situations and circumstances in life most worth living or dying for, often are on the side of the lines painted **<u>IMPOSSIBLE</u>?**

Doesn't it seem like these so-called impossible lines are the most difficult lines to cross or break? This is because most of these lines are psychological, cultural or spiritual. Unfortunately, many of these lines are not so easily detected. Especially when they are deeply rooted into our subconscious mind. Once these lines of behavior are constituted into the main frame of our subconscious mind they become masked by deeply embedded emotional responses that blur the line between who we really are and what is simply learned behavior on our part.

Fortunately, human history testifies to the fact that most of the so-called "impossible" lines in life can be crossed and broken; especially when we solicit God's help!

CROSSING LINES OF SCIENTIFIC IMPOSSIBILITIES

For centuries most people believed that the earth was flat. Don't forget that until Portuguese born Ferdinand Magellan sailed around the world and Christopher Columbus discovered America, it was unheard of to sail westward, as the accepted belief of the time was that if you did, you would fall off of the "flat" Earth. Not long after Columbus sailed west and Ferdinand Megallan sailed around the globe, and humanity crossed another "impossible" line and discovered that the Earth is actually round.

For centuries it was also assumed it was impossible for a man to walk on the moon. As we all know now, the American Astronaut Neil Armstrong crossed an impossible line when he landed on the moon in 1969 aboard the Apollo 11. Good thing he never got the memo that walking on the moon was "impossible."

**History proves mankind has created a habit
of crossing and breaking impossible lines.**

History definitely proves that mankind has made a habit of crossing previously impossible lines. Not only the impossible lines in the natural but also in the spiritual realm. Consider the lines between love and hate, between forgiveness and unforgiveness that have been crossed and broken, many times over.

A Pope and the Assassins Bullet

On May 13, 1981, would-be assassin Mehmet Ali shot Pope John Paul II at close range in St. Peter's Square. That night over 1 billion Catholics prayed and pleaded with God to save the Pope's life. The faithful gathered by the thousands inside St. Peter's square in a candlelight vigil to intercede for their beloved Pope's life. By sunrise, news spread that the hospitalized Pope was in stable condition to the relief of millions of Catholics.

Something else happened by sunrise as well . . . Mehmet Ali had likely become one of the most hated and despised men on Earth. His face was plastered on the television screens of most major news outlets. What most people do not realize is that the Pope's first official duty after he recovered was to cross the **line** between love and hate, forgiveness and unforgiveness by visiting the jail cell of the man who had tried to kill him. The photo of Pope John Paul II praying with his would be killer in his jail cell went viral. Many people were inspired by the Pope's actions to cross the line between forgiveness and unforgiveness in their own life.

The Line Behind the Red Curtain

What about the fall of the Soviet Union? Who ever thought that would ever happen? Was that not a line that seemed impossible to break or cross? Ask anyone who was alive during the Cold War and they will tell you without hesitation that they never expected to see the Soviet Union fall apart in their lifetime. Due to the belief and determination of so many courageous men and women, today we live in a world that is now free for several hundred million people; who lived under the tyranny of communist regimes behind the Red Curtain. Something most thought would be impossible, especially the people who lived behind the Red Curtain.

LONG WALK TO FREEDOM

Even more recently, we have saw an invisible line that existed for over 100 hundred years crossed that no one ever expected to be crossed. I am referring to the line between government run apartheid and freedom that was crossed on April 27, 1994 in the rainbow nation of South Africa. I am most excited about the crossing of this line because I was there when it happened. The mood of that day was a breathtaking mixture of somberness, fear and excitement as millions of South Africans stood in long lines for hours for a once-in-a-lifetime opportunity. They stood in line for the opportunity to cast their first vote for the first black presidential candidate in a country that had been ravaged by years of a very bloody apartheid system.

It was a **DREAM** come true for so many South Africans, and yet the dream was so fragile, that many feared the dream would not survive the night.

However, when Nelson Mandela was sworn in as South Africa's first black president on the 10th of May 1994, South Africans, along with the rest of the world, had just experienced the **turning of an "impossibility."** A multigenerational line most never expected to be broken or crossed in their lifetime had just been shattered into a million pieces. I watched from the comfort of my home in Pretoria the swearing ceremony of Nelson Mandela, which was attended by many world leaders and celebrities.

As you can see, it is possible to cross and break impossible lines.

But what about the impossible lines that you are facing?

The lines that seem to keep you from
living your life to its highest potential?

The lines that you wish you could cross and break
which are keeping you from living in freedom?

You know the lines I am referring to.

Is it possible to cross and break those lines?

The answer is YES!

But that brings up the question of HOW, doesn't it? Fortunately answering this question is the guiding beacon of this book. My goal is to show you a biblical pattern for breaking and jumping over invisible lines that are encroaching on your God given destiny. In order for me to do this effectively, I first need to introduce you to the concept of **"Bloodlines and Sidelines."**

CHAPTER TWO

BLOODLINES AND SIDELINES

For the life of the flesh is in the blood, and I have given it to you upon the altar to make atonement for your souls; for it is the blood that makes atonement for the soul.' Leviticus 17:11 (NKJV)

At the beginning of this writing I mentioned that life is full of lines. But they are no "lines" that affect human behavior and destiny like "Bloodlines and Sidelines." In this chapter we will discuss in detail these two categories of lines. We will define them, as well as make a clear distinction between the two.

BLOODLINES

Bloodlines by definition are **lines of direct descent through the blood**. This means that bloodlines are strictly "generational" and anything generational is deeply influenced by the "genetics" of the specific bloodline under scrutiny. This means that the genetic proclivities between different bloodlines will differ between specific family groups. This would explain why alcoholism maybe the genetic proclivity of one bloodline, while sexual abuse maybe the genetic proclivity most common to another family. Since bloodlines are genetically influenced, bloodline curses are the most difficult to break. But thank God that the blood of Jesus is more powerful than any satanic genetic proclivity attached to any natural ancestral line.

BLOOD = LIFE

The writer of the book of Leviticus makes a very important and revolutionary statement, "the life of the soul is in the blood." This is why the Prophet Isaiah called the shedding of the blood of Jesus, "the pouring of His soul unto death" (Isaiah 53:7-9). Both the life and soul of Jesus was in His blood. Consequently when Jesus shed His blood for us on the Cross-, He was truly giving us His life.

The more you study what the bible says about the blood the more you realize why there is no forgiveness of sin without the shedding of blood (Hebrews 9:22). This statement from the book of Hebrews also helps us to understand why the devil loves blood sacrifices in most satanic rituals. When I was deathly ill and in desperate need of healing, my heathen uncle took me to an African witchdoctor. The witchdoctor made several incisions in my body in order to draw blood so she could start her treatment. Perhaps this is why my deliverance from the devil's grip over my life took a face-to-face encounter with Jesus.

SOURCE OF BLOODLINE CURSES

Again the word of the Lord came to me, saying, 2 "Son of man, cause Jerusalem to know her abominations, 3 and say, 'Thus says the Lord God to Jerusalem: "Your birth and your nativity are from the land of Canaan; your father was an Amorite and your mother a Hittite. 4 As for your nativity, on the day you were born your navel cord was not cut, nor were you washed in water to cleanse you; you were not rubbed with salt nor wrapped in swaddling cloths. 5 No eye pitied you, to do any of these things for you, to have compassion on you; but you were thrown out into the open field, when you yourself were loathed on the day you were born. 6 "And **when I passed by you and saw you struggling in your own blood, I said to you in your blood, 'Live!' Yes, I said to you in your blood, 'Live!'** Ezekiel 16:1-6 (NKJV)

Here is the million-dollar question: What is the source of bloodline curses? The source of bloodline curses is our nativity or ancestral heritage. Any ancestral heritage can be traced from our fathers' or mothers' bloodline. These are the two progenitors that contribute greatly to our DNA or genetic profile. This is why today's courts of law use DNA testing to ascertain the paternity of a child in the middle of a custody battle. DNA results in most courts of law are considered irrefutable evidence. This is why we have to deal with a person's ancestral bloodlines before they "Jump the line" to effect deliverance from generational curses. This book will concentrate on helping you understand the spiritual technology for overturning generational bloodline curses through a simple but powerful prophetic act called "Jumping the line."

SIDELINES

Our study finalizes leads us to the subject of "Sidelines." I discovered "Sidelines" right after I started praying for people to "Jump the line" for the purpose of breaking generational curses. Many of the people I prayed experienced instant deliverance from things or addictions that they are struggled with for a long time. But some of the people were still struggling. I wondered what was going on in such cases. Soon after the Lord gave me a revelation.

The revelation came in the form of strong mental impression and I heard the words, "not every line is a bloodline, some lines are sidelines that some people are dealing with." As the spirit of revelation flooded my soul, the Lord showed me that bloodlines are "generational" whereas sidelines are "situational." I could hardly contain my excitement as truth flooded my soul. Suddenly I could explain some people whom "Jumping the line" did not seem to help. In such cases I was focusing on breaking generational bloodline curses, while ignoring the real problem they needed deliverance from.

To make my point clear let me give you a visual example of the stark difference between "Bloodlines and Sidelines." Johnny Carson comes from a family of alcoholics dating back to the seventh generation. Naturally Johnny Carson starts drinking heavily. This act is definitely generational. But one day Johnny Carson breaks his leg in a car accident. He is forced to wear a cast on his leg and is sidelined from playing football for six months. Do you see the difference? Drinking alcohol heavily is a generational curse in Johnny Carson's life but being unable to play football due to the accident is "situational." The latter is easier to overcome than the former. On the other hand if Johnny Carson has a bad attitude towards his injury, his bad attitude towards his injury may sideline him from getting back on the field and playing far longer than the injury to his leg.

"You're familiar with the command to the ancients, 'Do not murder.' I'm telling you that anyone who is so much as angry with a brother or sister is guilty of murder. Carelessly call a brother 'idiot!' and you just might find yourself hauled into court. Thoughtlessly yell 'stupid!' at a sister and you are on the brink of hellfire. The simple moral fact is that words kill. "This is how I want you to conduct yourself in these matters. If you enter your place of worship and, about to make an offering, you suddenly remember a grudge a friend has against you, abandon your offering, leave immediately, go to this friend and make things right. Then and only then, come back and work things out with God.
Matthew 5:21-24

As a matter of fact Johnny Carson's attitude towards his injury could actually produce several "Sidelines." For instance his negative attitude could lead to unforgiveness towards the other driver, low self esteem, self-pity, self-hatred or anger. Since the bible is very clear that our holy God will NOT use any person who harbors the above, Johnny Carson will be sidelined from being used by God until the above issues are properly dealt with. This book contains teaching on some "Sidelines" as well as some sample prayers about how to deal with "Sidelines." Our one-of-a-kind Mobile App contains articles on different sidelines and prayers for "Jumping over" sidelines that are standing in your path to complete freedom.

JUMP the LINE

CHAPTER THREE

UNDERSTANDING THE "MAN IN THE MIRROR"

But we all, with unveiled face, beholding as in a mirror the glory of the Lord,
are being transformed into the same image from glory to glory,
just as by the Spirit of the Lord.
2 Corinthians 3:18

For most of us, we have told ourselves at least once in life, "I will never act anything like my. . . dad, mom or someone else I am related to" because we did not like what we saw growing up. If only it was that simple. Come to think of it, the revelation contained in this book does make it simple, for the first time I might add. Unfortunately, for most of us, at least once in our life, one day we looked in the mirror and realized the reflection in the mirror is everything we had promised our self we would never be. We realize that we are doing some of the exact same things we swore to ourselves we would never do in life. And, if the truth be told, many of us are realizing that we demonstrating the same kind of genetic proclivities, prejudices and anti-Christ behaviors that we despised in our mothers, fathers, uncles, aunts and relatives. Sound familiar? If it does, you are not alone.

For most of us, these actions and behaviors seem to show up suddenly in our lives. However, the truth is they have always been there, we just did not see them. And that should not really be surprising. **We all become**

17

"conditioned" to the environment around us. In many cases, we behave and speak and respond just like the people we are surrounded by, yet we expect different outcomes.

We expect not to be poor, not to be abusive, not to be sick, not to be negative, not to be jealous or not to be entangled in addiction. Still, more often than not, we find ourselves engaging in the very same behaviors we find in our environment, the performance displayed by the people we are surrounded by.

Do not be deceived: "Bad company corrupts good morals." 1 Corinthians 15:33

So, part of changing the person in the mirror is to change your environment.

However, that is only part of the HOW; and it is the small part. The other part of the HOW, the big part, the part that will truly set you free, is understanding how your inherited genetic proclivities in your bloodline affect your life. **The most difficult lines to break or cross are "bloodlines."** Bloodlines are the reasons we are so connected mentally, emotionally and behaviorally to our family's past (specific mannerisms, actions and conduct). This is by far the primary reason there are certain areas of our life that seem impossible to change for the better.

For example, many people will tell you they despise their abusive fathers, mothers, aunts or uncles, but end up marrying people who resemble the pain from their past. They marry people exactly like the people they hated growing up around or repeating the same destructive relationships over and over again. Consider children who were raised by a parent who was emotionally closed off or detached – a parent who showed little or no positive loving affection. Or even worse, offered only negative reinforcement. Far too often, people who grew up in such an environment are now exposing their own children to the same level of emotional detachment and suffering they experienced themselves as children. How do you logically explain this?

I am sure you know of such situations. And, I'll bet in your mind these types of situations don't really make any sense. Doesn't it seem almost impossible for someone to repeat the very behaviors they despise? Unfortunately it happens all of the time for so many of us. The question is, "How can we explain this behavior?"

SIMPLE . . . BLOODLINES!

Think about it like this: Since our bloodlines, to a large degree, can actually govern our subconscious behavior. It's not inconceivable then to admit that in most cases our past is driving and controlling our present. Specifically, the way we think, the way we feel, the way we act and the manner in which we make decisions on a daily basis.

Bloodlines are the primary reasons so many of us find ourselves in repetitive cycles of failure, divorce, betrayal, financial misfortune and sickness. And, far too often, no matter how hard we work at avoiding and overcoming these destructive areas of our life, they continue to plague us.

SO, WHAT IS ACTUALLY GOING ON HERE?

Most of the repetitive issues that we struggle with, which are not environmental, are actually generational – issues that stem from the past of our immediate family as well as our forefathers. The primary culprit behind many of these repetitive issues is a highly **"compromised generational bloodline."** You might be wondering what I mean by the word, generational. Let me explain. I am referring to family generations, which are,

"A group of humans in a line of descent from a common ancestor."

Simply stated, familial generations are a line (lineage) of ancestors. For example:

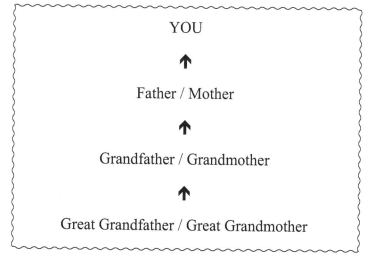

YOU

↑

Father / Mother

↑

Grandfather / Grandmother

↑

Great Grandfather / Great Grandmother

A few important facts you may want to know about family generations:

1. We all have two specific family generations, one that connects us to our father's lineage and one that connects us to our mother's lineage.

2. Our connection to our family generations is partly environmental and partly genetic. As I have already shared, part of our present day mannerisms, thinking and behavior is connected to our environment. And for most of us, our environment, both past and present, has strongly impacted our family. At the same time, we all carry DNA similar to (and connected to) the DNA of our ancestors or progenitors. It's an immutable fact that we are connected to our ancestral lineage genetically. I will have more to say on this in later chapters.

3. There is always good in any generation. It is important to always remember that regardless of who your ancestors were and where they came from, they passed on to you some pretty good stuff! I am sure there are certain aspects of your behavior, thinking and appearance that you are proud of. In fact, you are probably proud of certain things you can do that few people in the world can do as well as you. Never forget to be thankful for the good stuff you got from your ancestors. The **"good stuff you received from your ancestors is part of your godly heritage."**

4. But we ALL have the "other stuff" (the bad stuff), too. Specifically, I am referring to certain aspects of our behavior, thinking and appearance that, we are less than thrilled about.

As you already know, any aspect of our environment that is connected to our family generations can be changed, improved and upgraded. It is within your own personal power to change attitudes, routines, habits and even individuals within your environment. Of course, this is sometimes easier said than done. Still, it is possible. Those are lines YOU CAN cross. Hopefully the revelation contained in this book will help fuel your faith to "Jump over lines" that represent things you need to overcome.

But what about the behaviors connected to your family generations you cannot seem to change, no matter what you do. Well, these are not environmental they are genetic. Unfortunately, these are not behaviors YOU can change at a drop of the hat. They are too deeply rooted in your ancestors' genetic past. Most importantly the genetic proclivities contained in your ancestral DNA has now been passed down to you....deeply encroached inside what you now call your DNA.

**I am serious . . . YOU CANNOT change
these behaviors through wishful thinking!**

You can get ahead of them maybe, for a while, but you will revert to the original deeply programed behavior. No matter what you do in your own strength, in time, you will fail and ultimately lose hope, give up and abandon yourself to live with whatever behavior it is that is holding you back from experiencing the complete freedom that Christ promises us. If you happen to know what I am talking about, then you know how depressing it is to feel that you are not in control of a portion of your life.

It almost feels like there is a curse on you!

The take-away here is this: *There are some lines you just can't cross in your own strength.*

However, that does not mean you cannot be free!!!

I know that sounds contradictory, or you might think there was a typo here in the text. Believe me that is not the case. I said you can't do it . . . but that does not mean it can't be done. In fact, it has already been done for you.

**Yes, that is right . . . it has been done for you...through the blood of
Jesus Christ!**

JUMP the LINE

CHAPTER FOUR
HEAVEN ON EARTH

Your kingdom come. Your will be done On earth as it is in heaven. Matthew 6:10

If you know Jesus, I am almost certain that you have had a life-changing encounter of some kind. One where you knew instantly that something very powerful and life changing had taken place inside your spirit. Most likely, peace and joy full of glory rushed into your soul and for the first time in your life, you felt clean from the inside out. For the first few months, you were probably running on the spiritual adrenaline that comes with receiving Jesus as your personal Lord and Savior for the very first time.

Hopefully, that spiritual adrenaline is still with you . . . and has increased with time.

However, that is not the case for everyone. Many believers I meet often lose that initial spark of life they felt and experienced when they gave their life to Christ. For some, the daily grind of life at home and in the marketplace has taken its toll and they find themselves wondering why they seem to struggle so much when Jesus promised them a life of abundance in the Bible.

If this sounds somewhat familiar, you are not alone. This is something most believers struggle with, from time to time. I remember, many years ago, I used to ask myself why this is so common in the lives of believers. I would pray and ask, "Lord, why is it that so many believers struggle so much with life here on earth? Lord, why are so many believers overwhelmed by life's daily challenges, when the Bible promises them so much?"

Then, it was revealed to me that for most believers, one of the reasons they struggle here on Earth is because they are missing something. Something critical to their faith walk; specifically, they are missing the climate of **HEAVEN** in their space of real estate.

LET ME EXPLAIN

When you read the words of Jesus in all the Gospels, it's clear that God intended for us to have **HEAVEN HERE ON EARTH**. However, that is not exactly what so many believers have been taught. It would seem that most believers have been taught the "Gospel of Salvation," rather than the "Gospel of the Kingdom." And there is a difference . . . **A BIG ONE!**

In this manner, therefore, pray: Our Father in heaven, Hallowed be Your name. 10 Your kingdom come. Your will be done on earth as it is in heaven. 11 Give us this day our daily bread.12 And forgive us our debts, as we forgive our debtors. 13 And do not lead us into temptation, But deliver us from the evil one. For Yours is the kingdom and the power and the glory forever. Amen Matthew 6:9-13

The **"Gospel of Salvation"** is focused on saving people from their sins and getting them to heaven as the primary goal. However, getting to heaven is not the endgame, rather it's the first step towards a personal relationship with our Lord and Savior.

The **"Gospel of the Kingdom,"** on the other hand, is a gospel that is focused on saving people from their sins, while bringing HEAVEN down to EARTH. Amazingly, many believers have not been exposed to the Gospel of the Kingdom, and that is one of the primary reasons why so many blood-washed Christians are struggling so much to excel in life.

Too often, it seems, believers have been conditioned by teaching that encourages followers of Jesus to suffer through life while they wait to die and go to HEAVEN. The truth is that is not what Jesus taught! Not even close. The truth is that Jesus Christ taught something completely different. He taught a Gospel of the Kingdom that believes NOT in STRUGGLING through LIFE. Rather, the Gospel of the Kingdom teaches that as believers, we are to EXCEL in every area of life . . . here on earth . . . experiencing HEAVEN ON EARTH through the power of the Holy Spirit.

WHAT JESUS PROMISED

To be clear, I am not suggesting that believers will never be challenged or faced with hardship. All believers who live a godly life will at some point in their life face persecution. Jesus clearly teaches that throughout the Gospels. However, when such situations arise, Jesus taught us that the Kingdom and all its glory is on our side through the power of the Holy Spirit. Jesus' promise to all believers is that **Heaven will invade Earth.**

Jesus promised all believers: that God will show up in your life. He wants to show up, and if He is not showing up in your life REGULARLY, then heaven is not invading your piece of Earth! Hopefully, the "explosive" information contained in this book and our very robust "Jump The Line" Mobile App (download it @ www.francismyles.com) will help bridge the GAP between your piece of EARTH and HEAVEN!

JUMP the LINE

JUMP the LINE

CHAPTER FIVE
THE "REAL DEAL" ABOUT JESUS

By now I am sure you may have figured out that what I am sharing in this book is centered on being able to cross over the lines in life that keep you from moving forward. If you are reading this book, I know you and I have at least one thing in common . . . **we both have a desire for a better life than we are living now.**

Come on, if you are reading this book right now I know YOU KNOW what I am talking about.

**Don't you feel like you were created
for something better?**

**Don't you feel that there is more to life that
you are just not getting?**

If the answer to either one of those questions is yes, then you and I share the same history. Many years ago my answer to both of those questions was yes. However, just like with everything in life, the biggest answers always lie within the question of <u>HOW?</u>

Here is my answer to you . . . you have to cross the line between you and the ONE individual in human history who made the audacious claim of being the only begotten Son of God. **He had one consuming message... "Bringing Heaven on Earth, while helping us conquer all of our personal demons!"**

He so believed that you and I can have HEAVEN HERE ON EARTH... that He died for all mankind on a Cross stained with His precious blood. There is no person more talked about in human history and, subsequently, more misunderstood than JC.

Who Himself bore our sins in His own body on the tree, that we, having died to sins, might live for righteousness—by whose stripes you were healed.
1 Peter 2:24

I know it may seem like some lines are too hard to cross, and I promise you I will show you how you can cross those impossible lines. However, there is **one line** . . . you can cross **right now** . . . it's not an impossible line to cross. It is the line between you and freedom. It is the line that keeps you from peace. It is the line that keeps you from what you were created to be. It's the line standing between you and the promise to live forever in heaven.

While there are many lines we all need to cross in our life, there is one particular "LINE" that <u>I KNOW</u> will have the most positive impact.

<u>It's the line between you and God!</u>

But your iniquities have separated you from your God;
And your sins have hidden His face from you,
So that He will not hear. Isaiah 59:2

It is not the line between you and religion that matters....
Religion is like feasting on stale bread when the aroma of "FRESH" bread is beckoning us.

If you are like most people, this is a line that you may be most scared of, because you don't know what to expect or whether God will accept you or not. For some of you, the line between you and placing your faith in Jesus Christ may also be scary if you have spent most of your life running from God. But you need not be afraid. God loves you a million times more than you love yourself. The reason He sent His Son into the world to die on the cross is so you can have HEAVEN HERE ON EARTH.

As one who crossed that line many years ago, I discovered the PEACE and JOY that I never thought was humanly possible. In the Bible Jesus promises those who place their faith in Him a life of abundance. When you read the words of Jesus in all the Gospels, it's very clear that Jesus intended for mankind to have HEAVEN HERE ON EARTH.

A thief is only there to steal and kill and destroy. I came so they can have real and eternal life, more and better life than they ever dreamed of. John 10:10

I assure you that God wants you just as you are. You are not too dirty or sinful for God to embrace. Will you give your life to Jesus right now? Are you ready to experience HEAVEN ON EARTH? It starts by accepting Jesus as your personal Lord and Savior. It is about making a choice to ENTER into a **"REALationship"** with God through His Son. It is not a choice; to live by man made rules or become religious nutcase. NO it's NOT!

If that's what you were told, "You" have been misinformed. Jesus is not about performance and rules; He is about living under His grace and mercy through faith in His finished work on the cross.

Now God has us where he wants us, with all the time in this world and the next to shower grace and kindness upon us in Christ Jesus. Saving is all his idea, and all his work. All we do is trust him enough to let him do it. It's God's gift from start to finish! We don't play the major role. If we did, we'd probably go around bragging that we'd done the whole thing! No, we neither make nor save ourselves. God does both the making and saving.
Ephesians 2:7-9

Please pray this prayer out loud: "Heavenly Father, I believe that Jesus Christ is the Son of God, that He died on the cross and then rose from the dead so that I can walk in the newness of life. I ask Jesus to come and live inside my heart. Thank You for forgiving me of all my sins. Amen."

If you prayed that prayer, Jesus just came into your heart through the power of the Holy Spirit. Establishing a relationship with Jesus is the beginning of experiencing HEAVEN ON EARTH.... which Jumping the Line is all about.

But **JUMPING THE LINE** is not just about saying a prayer!

Jesus never said to pray a prayer; He said "FOLLOW ME!" So that is the decision for you made here; not to say some words and leave behind the BEST PART of EXPERIENCING HEAVEN ON EARTH. **FOLLOWING JESUS CHRIST!**

JUMP the LINE

CHAPTER SIX
HOW DID WE GET TO
THIS POINT ANYWAY?

And when I passed by you and saw you rolling about in your blood, I said to you in your blood, Live! Yes, I said to you still in your natal blood, Live! Ezekiel 16:6 (AMP)

In order to fully grasp bloodlines, it is important to understand the origin of bloodlines. So, a quick history lesson is in order.

The first bloodline was created through Adam and Eve, just after God created the Earth. When God created Adam and Eve, they were both created in God's own image and likeness. Since the phenomenon known as "likeness" is a "genetic function;" we can safely say that Adam and Eve had a pure and uncorrupted bloodline, containing many of God's invisible attributes.

Then God said, "Let Us make man in Our image, according to Our likeness; let them have dominion over the fish of the sea, over the birds of the air, and over the cattle, over all the earth and over every creeping thing that creeps on the earth."
Genesis 1:26 (KJV)

Interestingly, the Hebrew word for the word "image" used in the Bible is "TZELEM," which literally means "an exact representation, resemblance and manifestation of the original." So, it is clear mankind was initially created to be the exact representation, resemblance and manifestation of God.

What is critical to understand here is that when God created Adam and Eve in His image, God established a bloodline with humanity that was based on righteousness, life, freedom and perfection. Ultimately, giving humanity the ability to partake and enjoy Heaven on Earth. Adam and Eve were children of the Most High God in every sense of the word. They both carried the DNA of God in their genes.

In order to keep mankind's bloodline pure, God clearly instructed Adam and Eve NOT to eat from the Tree of the Knowledge of Good and Evil. In fact, God made it abundantly clear that the consequence in doing so, recorded in Genesis Chapter2, was that in the day they ate from the Tree of the Knowledge of Good and Evil they would surely die.

> *God commanded the Man, "You can eat from any tree in the garden,*
> *except from the Tree-of-Knowledge-of-Good-and-Evil. Don't eat from it.*
> *The moment you eat from that tree, you're dead." Genesis 2:16-17*

Unfortunately, Adam and Eve made a conscious decision NOT to obey the instructions of God. They chose to eat from the Tree of the Knowledge of Good and Evil and, in so doing, they **crossed a line** that should never have been crossed. Their foolish choice resulted in a number of consequences, including being forced to vacate the Garden of Eden and having to provide for themselves. They started enduring pain and hardships they could have avoided had they not crossed the line God specifically warned them about.

However, those consequences were small in comparison to the break in the bloodline with God. What is important to understand here is that when Adam and Eve crossed God's **forbidden line**, they severed their direct connection with God. Sin entered into their once pure and uncorrupted bloodline, corrupting and destroying it beyond repair.

Essentially, **they traded** . . .
righteousness, life, freedom and **perfection**
for **sin, death, slavery and failure.**

Adam and Eve broke the bloodline with God!

Ever since, humanity has been doing the same every day. But you do have a choice. You can choose to embrace by faith the finished work of Christ on the cross. You can choose to renounce your spiritual allegiance to your corrupted ancestral bloodlines and replace them with the incorruptible bloodline of our Jewish, Messiah, Jesus Christ of Nazareth.

TEMPTATION IS A CHOICE

At the beginning of our journey I told you that life is full of lines. Lines we are supposed to cross and those we shouldn't. And yet how many times have we all crossed lines that we knew we shouldn't have? This brings up an important question I believe I must answer right now. In those times when you have crossed lines you know you shouldn't have...

**Did the devil make you do it or
was it just part of the plan of God?**

The truth is . . . none of these! And how do I know this? I know this because of a major revelation of truth in the book of James, specifically Chapter 1, verses 13 -15.

Let no one say when he is tempted, "I am tempted by God"; for God cannot be tempted by evil, nor does He Himself tempt anyone. [14] But each one is tempted when he is drawn away by his own desires and enticed. [15] Then, when desire has conceived, it gives birth to sin; and sin, when it is full-grown, brings forth death. (KJV)

The passage of Scripture above clearly puts the responsibility of every line you cross, good or bad, squarely on your shoulders. Why is this so? It is because God created you and me with **FREE WILL**. That means we choose our own destiny.

It also means:

- **Life is full of choices.**
- **The devil does not "make us do it."**
- **Temptation is a choice.**
- **Yes, the devil steals from us, but we MUST be responsible to take our destiny back.**

Unfortunately, everywhere I travel around the world, it seems most people I meet just don't get this. Specifically, that all of us become a product of the choices we make. And that includes choices connected to how we respond to temptation.

All temptation, regardless of the pressure or difficulty connected to it, is ALWAYS a choice we have to make.

Let's make this real, shall we? The **DEVIL** is a **MASTER** of the art and science of tempting humanity. Let's not forget that he was successful in deceiving Adam and Eve into thinking that crossing a forbidden line would bring them pleasure and not pain. Instead of the pleasure, Satan had promised, what Adam and Eve actually received was **sin, diseases, fear, shame, addictions and all kinds of pain**. For sure, they did not get what they were promised. **Sound familiar?**

YOU DO HAVE A CHOICE

Sometimes I wish that God would tell us what to do and we would have no choice but to obey, thus avoiding temptation all together. But God loves us so much that He gave us the right to choose. The right to choose **ALWAYS** includes choosing whether or not we fall into temptation. Not to fear, though.

Even though the Devil is quite experienced in tempting people that does not leave us powerless to his tricks and the onslaught of peer pressure. You can overcome all temptation through Christ who strengthens you. But what do we do when we fall into temptation and feel like we can't get out of it? This is a very good question; because, you see, we are not the only ones with a choice. **God has a choice, too.**

CHAPTER SEVEN

AND, GOD HAD A CHOICE AS WELL

Immediately after Adam and Eve crossed the **forbidden line**, they were disconnected from the glory of God. God's warning that they would die the day they ate of the tree of the knowledge of good and evil, came true. The clothing of God's glory that Adam and Eve were very accustomed left them and they immediately felt naked. And what was God's response to their act of treason?

After Adam and Eve had disobeyed God by eating from the forbidden tree, in the cool of the day God walked into the Garden looking for them. When they heard the movement of His presence they hid behind the leaves of a tree (since then, men and women from all walks of life have tried unsuccessfully to run away from the presence of God). "Adam where are you?" was the passionate cry of God as He sought to restore the broken fellowship.

And with that broken fellowship, God had a choice.

Even though Adam and Eve had disappointed Him...

God chose to bet on mankind.

Genesis 3:7

35

Please remember that after Adam and Eve sinned, their pure bloodline was broken. This changed the family dynamic forever. No longer pure, they were disconnected from God. Adam and Eve, along with all of humanity, immediately moved from being "sons" of God to "servants" of God; from innocence to sinful. This left God with a choice – **to let us be servants**, forever distanced from Him, or to somehow restore us to **our rightful place as sons**.

Thankfully, **God decided to bet on us.** And it should be no surprise that God bet on us, because His original intent was to have a people on Earth He could be close to . . . a people created in His own image and likeness. God wanted spirit-sons in earthly bodies that He could fellowship with.

Ultimately, God's solution to restore us to Sonship was the only viable option available to Him that did not thwart His original intent. God's ultimate solution to the sin problem in mankind was to offer a pure sacrifice on the Cross to restore the broken and polluted bloodline. So in sending Jesus to die for us, God was able to restore humanity to Sonship.
What I have just shared is something most believers understand; however, my observation is most believers really don't get it.

I know I didn't until I learned a BIG lesson in the BIG state of Texas.

Before sharing my BIG Texas experience, that can only be described as a face-to-face encounter with Jesus, I need to clarify something first. Specifically, **God's primary intent for creating mankind.**

God's Primary Intent

As I have already mentioned, God's original intent when He created Earth and mankind was to establish a **pure royal bloodline of sons** of the Kingdom who can advance the dominion of His heavenly Kingdom into every sphere of human endeavor. God's original intent also involves us having direct access to the Heavenly Father, while enjoying Heaven on Earth.

Through the blood of Jesus that was shed on the **"Cross,"** the bloodline between humanity and God was restored. Consequently it should be no surprise that any of us would have an encounter with Jesus if our heart is set on seeking the Kingdom of God and His righteousness.
Nevertheless, when we encounter Jesus through a supernatural experience like the one I am about to share with you, this can be quite a challenge for most people to accept. I totally understand human skepticism towards the

And God Had a Choice as Well...!

supernatural –trust me, it is also hard for the one receiving the supernatural encounter to initially accept it, too! However, should it be so difficult to believe that we all can encounter **Jesus here on Earth?**

Rather, shouldn't it make perfect sense?

In my many years of apostolic service, I have traveled to many nations, I have discovered that most people, regardless of their confession of faith, at least once in their life have felt a presence they couldn't explain, usually described as a voice "speaking to their heart." Guess what, that "voice" is the presence of God trying to invade their life. This is the beginning of Heaven on Earth.

It's the beginning of a "REALationship."

Unfortunately, many miss this primary intention of our Father God. If you carefully read through the first few chapters of the book of Genesis, it is abundantly clear that God created mankind for relationship. After man's royal bloodline was corrupted by sin, mankind was separated from God. However, a direct connection with Father God has been reestablished for all of us through the blood of Jesus that was shed on the Cross.

This brings up a profound question, doesn't it . . . how do we access that relationship? Obviously, religion alone isn't enough. Remember, man, not God, created religion. Religion is fallen man's attempt to reach God through the arm of the flesh. This why religion kills, while a relationship with Christ gives life. I have had many Christians say to me, "I have accepted Jesus Christ as my personal Savior and still I feel somewhat distant from God. I really don't feel like I am in a relationship with God. What can I do? Wasn't accepting Jesus as my personal Lord and Savior enough?"

When I am asked questions like this, my answer is always the same, "Christ dying on the Cross was most definitely enough. However, just saying a prayer and going to church will not bring you into a very robust relationship with Jesus, any more than reciting vows at a wedding will guarantee a successful marriage." For most people, that analogy makes logical sense. However, there is more. Even though the blood of Jesus restored our long lost royal bloodline for all of us, after accepting Jesus as their personal Lord and Savior, most people still live and operate on the **unrestored side of the bloodline.** Not sure what I mean? Let me explain. Rather, I will let Jesus explain.

JUMP the LINE

CHAPTER EIGHT

MY ENCOUNTER...
THE BACKSTORY

If you have ever heard the expression, "Everything is BIGGER in Texas," I can tell you the statement is true. How do I know this? Because of my personal experience; one in particular that was VERY BIG for me and VERY PERSONAL.

May 18, 2009

MY ENCOUNTER WITH JESUS IN TEXAS

It all began around 9:00pm to the best of my recollection. I was in Dallas, Texas, to meet with a small group of Christian businessmen. We had agreed to meet at the Gaylord Resort, which is located on the outskirts of the city. If you have ever been to the Gaylord, then you know it is a very large resort with just about any amenity you can think of. My point; the resort is really big! It is so big, in order to accommodate parking for all of the guests, the resort built a multi-story parking garage adjacent to the main entrance of the resort.

When I arrived, I pulled into the parking garage and was able to immediately find a spot on the first floor. After parking, I grabbed my briefcase, locked my car and walked through the parking garage towards the main entrance of the resort. The walk from the parking garage to the main entrance was more than a few feet. I only bring this up because that is where I got lost. Yes, lost in the glory!

During dinner with my businessmen friends from Colorado, I realized that I had forgotten something in the car. Don't you just hate that? I know I do; well, at least I used to. It doesn't bother me anymore. In fact, I kind of look forward to it now. Here is why.

I quickly walked back to my parked car, unlocked the driver's door, grabbed whatever it was I had forgotten (I don't even remember what it was now). I locked the car door and proceeded to walk back to the main entrance of the resort. And, just as I left the parking garage . . . it happened. This is when I got lost in the glory cloud. To say I was "ambushed" by the presence of God is probably not the best way to describe it, even though I was completely taken off guard. Remember, I just went back to the car to grab something I had forgotten. I certainly did not expect to have an encounter with Jesus on the way back.

I can only describe my experience like this. Imagine taking a step forward and immediately feeling like you walked into an atmosphere that enveloped you with overpowering liquid love and, at the same time, the air around you was charged with a thick layer of the glory and presence of God. In an instant, my mind became clear as crystal. I was captivated and in awe of what I was experiencing . . . all at the same time.

Simultaneously, I heard a voice so strong and so loud in my heart it seemed almost audible. The voice came from Jesus . . . and He simply said this, "Let's take a walk." So what did I do then? What do you think? I took a walk with Jesus. I cannot tell you much about the walk itself, only that when this encounter was over I had somehow made my way from just outside the parking garage to the main entrance of the resort. This is what I mean by getting lost in the glory because I don't remember anything about my trip back to the resort.

What I can tell you is that on my walk I received a supernatural download from heaven. **Jesus gave me a stunning revelation on how to break generational curses, addictions, repetitive behavior cycles and genetic bondage <u>permanently</u>**. Moreover, it was revealed to me how anyone can experience Heaven on Earth and bridge the relational gap with God so many of us struggle with.

GENETIC SALVATION

After hearing the words, "Let's take a walk," Jesus declared to me *"It's TIME, It's TIME, It's TIME."* *"Time for what LORD?"* I asked. *"It's TIME for My People around the World to Experience 'Genetic Salvation.'"* The Lord declared. I can still remember feeling somewhat stunned, puzzled and confused. I had never heard of the expression "Genetic Salvation." I consider myself a tenacious student of the Word of God with a doctorate in Theology and Biblical studies to prove it. But I had never head of the term "Genetic Salvation" ever! Jesus continued, *"'Genetic Salvation'* is when the finished work of Christ on the Cross is applied by faith to the healing of my people's broken down genetics, so that the children of God can inherit the Messiah's bloodline and overturn every generational curse attached to their ancestral bloodlines."

BIBLICAL GENETICS

"Son, I am going to teach you Biblical Genetics," Jesus continued with a voice that seemed to send shockwaves through my entire being. And at that moment, Jesus began to reveal to me what Biblical Genetics was all about. My lesson began with an explanation of the word GENERATIONS. The LORD showed me that the word **GENERATIONS** is made up of two words actually . . . **"GENE and RATIONS."**

By definition a **"Gene"** is the basic unit of heredity in all-living organisms. All living things depend on genes. Genes hold the information to build and maintain an organism's cells and pass genetic traits to the offspring. The word **"Ration,"** as the Lord showed me, refers to "a portion designated to a person or group." The word ration literally means the apportioning of a ration or portion.

What I immediately understood was that for all of us, our **GENE-RATIONS** have positives and negatives traits connected to them. And when it comes to the negative traits, they can be likened to a "CURSE." By definition a "curse" can best be defined as:

☐ *Something causing misery or death*

☐ *A hex or evil spell*

☐ *An appeal to some supernatural power to inflict evil on someone or some group*

So the negative effects of our lineage or bloodline are in essence **"Generational Curses." These are curses attached to the ration of genes we inherited from our progenitors.** To be clear, a generational curse, therefore, is a negative and destructive subconscious behavior pattern that is attached to the ration of genes we inherited from our ancestors. What is of note here is that *generational curses* do not track learned behavior; rather, they trace patterns of behavior on a subconscious and genetic level. Simply stated all generational curses greatly influence a person's genetics and DNA.

What I think is important to realize is that even though the concept of generational curses may be new to you, the truth of the matter is that "generational curses" are as old as human history. This is evidenced by the fact that generational curses have affected the lives of some of the spiritual giants of the Bible.

LIKE FATHER LIKE SON!

Then a famine came to the land. Abram went down to Egypt to live; it was a hard famine. As he drew near to Egypt, he said to his wife, Sarai, "Look. We both know that you're a beautiful woman. When the Egyptians see you they're going to say, 'Aha! That's his wife!' and kill me. But they'll let you live. Do me a favor: tell them you're my sister. Because of you, they'll welcome me and let me live." Genesis 12:10-13

For example, when Abraham first went down to Egypt, he coerced his wife to say that she was his sister instead of his wife. Fast-forward and you will see the same behavioral tendency in his son Isaac. I can guarantee you that Abraham never coached his son to behave this way. The information and proclivity for this type of behavior was already stored in the DNA, Isaac inherited from his father. The Bible records that when Isaac was confronted with the same challenges his father had faced many years earlier, he acted exactly like his father Abraham. Isaac told his wife (Rebekah) to tell her admirers that she was not his wife but his sister.

So Isaac dwelt in Gerar. ⁷ And the men of the place asked about his wife. And he said, "She is my sister"; for he was afraid to say, "She is my wife," because he thought, "lest the men of the place kill me for Rebekah, because she is beautiful to behold." ⁸ Now it came to pass, when he had been there a long time, that Abimelech king of the Philistines looked through a window, and saw, and there was Isaac, showing endearment to Rebekah his wife. ⁹ Then Abimelech called Isaac and said, "Quite obviously she is your wife; so how could you say, 'She is my sister'?" Isaac said to him, "Because I said, 'Lest I die on account of her.'" Genesis 26:6-9

As I am sure you can imagine, by this point I was completely overwhelmed. Nevertheless, Jesus was far from finished with me. At this point in "my walk," the Lord told me something I will never forget. He said, "Unless My children get a supernatural blood transfusion they will fail to extinguish the genetic corruption in their bloodline."

"Unless we get a supernatural blood transfusion we will fail to extinguish the genetic corruption in our bloodlines."

As my mind was reeling with the words Jesus just spoke to me, Luke 19:10 started to flash in my mind, **"The Son of man has come to seek and save that which was lost."**

Then, Jesus began to speak to me again, this time asking me a question, "What did you think I meant when I said this to My disciples?" Before I could answer, Jesus continued, "This Scripture is a *complete description of My assignment to the world*. I am the Last Adam as such I came to seek and save "everything" that was lost by the first Adam. Did you know that apart from Me, Adam and Eve were the only two humans who were born with flawless DNA and a pure bloodline?" Again, before I could answer, Jesus spoke to me. He took me to the book of Genesis and took me through Genesis 1:26.

Likeness: A Genetic Function

Then God said, "Let Us make man in Our image, according to Our likeness; let them have dominion over the fish of the sea, over the birds of the air, and over the cattle, over all the earth and over every creeping thing that creeps on the earth." Genesis 1:26 (KJV)

And Genesis 5:1-3,

This is the book of the generations of Adam. In the day that God created man, in the likeness of God made he him; ² male and female created he them; and blessed them, and called their name Adam, in the day when they were created. ³ And Adam lived an hundred and thirty years, and begat a son in his own likeness, after his image; and called his name Seth. (KJV)

Through these two passages of Scripture, Jesus emphasized to me that man was created in the image and likeness of God. He shared with me that "image" in the text refers to man's spirit because God is a Spirit. As

Jesus continued, He clarified to me that the word **"Likeness"** is a **"Genetic Function."** "What makes a child look or behave like its parents? It is 'Genes.' Genes control the phenomenon known as 'Likeness,'" Jesus replied. This statement is true even if you ask any genetic scientist.

When Jesus revealed this to me, the fifth chapter of Genesis took on a whole new meaning. The book of Genesis is by far my most favorite book in the Bible. I have read Genesis many times but I had never seen what the Lord revealed to me that night. It had not dawned on me until then that Genesis 5:1-3 contains the account of the most **destructive genetic degeneration or mutation** in recorded human history. It was essentially the beginning of the phenomenon commonly known as generational curses.

In Genesis 5:1, the Bible tells us that Adam and Eve were created in God's likeness. In other words, they carried the imprint of God's likeness on their genes. They both had the DNA of God flowing through their veins that governed their personality profile, internal motivations and personal destiny. **They were essentially the perfect human specimens. They carried in their blood the "holy grail" of genetic science, "the flawless gene!"**

However, when Adam and Eve fell into **"Sin"** they lost the flawless **DNA** of God, and in the process, corrupted their once pure bloodline for all humanity. By the time you get to Genesis 5:3 something tragic has happened. When Adam and Eve gave birth to their son Seth, he was born in "Adams" fallen image and likeness. This means that Seth's genetic profile was of a lower quality based upon the DNA of fallen sinful man, rather than the flawless DNA of God that Adam was created with.

THE LAST ADAM

Consequently, a Savior was needed on planet earth who could restore both the DNA of God, as well as establish another pure and uncorrupted bloodline or gene pool. Mankind was in desperate need of a new kind of "genetic pool;" a genetic pool without blemishes. Things don't end wrong they start wrong! So you cannot start with a corrupted gene pool and expect to produce a flawless specimen of human being. Did you get that? Please read this again, slowly and carefully . . .

A Savior was needed on planet earth who could restore both the DNA of God, as well as establish another pure and uncorrupted bloodline or gene pool.

Jesus clearly revealed to me that He shed His blood on the Cross and lived a Sinless Life not only to enable humanity to get to heaven . . . but to also enable us to experience Heaven on Earth. His shed blood not only washed our sins away; it also became the basis for restoring the long-lost DNA and Bloodline of God. Consequently the birth of Jesus Christ foreshadowed the arrival of a pure and uncorrupted bloodline that could be used to give birth to a "new race of people who have never existed on planet earth before." The Apostle Paul calls this new holy race generated from the blood of Jesus, "the new creation" (2 Cor 5:17) and saint Peter refers to them as the "holy nation and royal priesthood" (1 Peter 2:9). The blood of Jesus (Yeshua) restored our ability to connect directly with God and experience Heaven on Earth.

Are you ready for a "Heaven on Earth" lifestyle?

Unfortunately, for most of us being able to connect directly with God and experience Heaven on Earth seems to be out of reach. Not because it is impossible; rather, because most Christians, even after they accept Jesus as their personal Lord and Savior, still live and operate on the unrestored side of the bloodline. They continue to identify more with their ancestral bloodline more than the bloodline of Christ. Hopefully this book will change all of this.

JUMP the LINE

JUMP the LINE

CHAPTER NINE

A BIG QUESTION

How can we have **Heaven on Earth** if it seems like we are constantly haunted by the past? An important question, don't you think? For the record, I wish I could tell you that Christians are not subject to the genetic corruption I have shared with you. I also wish I could say that born-again believers cannot be negatively affected by generational curses. Unfortunately, that is not the case. The truth is, anywhere I have traveled, which is all over the world, I have met believers from all walks of life and all levels of faith, who are living and operating on the unrestored side of the bloodline.

My people are destroyed for lack of knowledge: because thou hast rejected knowledge, I will also reject thee, that thou shalt be no priest to me: seeing thou hast forgotten the law of thy God, I will also forget thy children. Hosea 4:6 (KJV)

When I reference people who are living on the "unrestored side of the bloodline" I am talking about good people, righteous people, Bible-believing people . . . men and women who have forsaken it all to follow Jesus. Furthermore, I personally know what it is like to be a slave to the past indiscretions of my forefathers . . . AS A BELIEVER in Christ nonetheless.

Not long after I made the decision to follow Jesus, I began to notice patterns of behavior in my life that were reminiscent of proclivities that I had observed in my immediate family members that I despised intensely. Nevertheless I was unable to overcome these same genetic tendencies in my own strength. Consequently I found myself engaging in the same type of behavior I so deeply despised.

My generational curse was deeply rooted anger that was so volatile, even the smallest irritation could cause me to lose my temper at a moment's notice. I would blow my fuse so quickly that I would be unable to control the tsunami of anger that gushed out of me. As is the case with generational curses, every time I would lose control, I found myself feeling very guilty in the aftermath. I felt hopeless and unable to change my shameful behavior. All the while the Holy Spirit continue to testify to my spirit that I was a born-again child of God and yet there was a side of me that was so unlike Jesus! It was not until I began to live and operate on the **RESTORED** side of the bloodline that I found peace and freedom from the anger that haunted my family for generations.

So, again I bring up the question,

How can we have Heaven on Earth if we are haunted by the past?

The answer is quite simple really, even though it may not always be so easy to live it out in practice — live and operate on the **RESTORED** side of the bloodline. I know that brings up the question of **HOW** again, doesn't it? Specifically, how can we overturn, reverse and destroy the demonically engineered patterns of behavior in our lives that keep us from living in total victory? I want you to know that contained in the pages of this book, is a **divine solution** we all have access to that can **destroy any genetic interference that is caused by demonic manipulation of our genes and bloodline** . . . I promise you!

A SOLUTION THAT WORKS EVERY TIME!

Only a light wind, gently brushing against my skin reminded me that I was still on Earth. Lost, somewhere between the parking garage and main entrance of the Gaylord Resort, my spirit was still vibrating with a heartfelt excitement and awe. I have an idea as to how Moses felt spending forty days and nights in the glory of God. Still, I could hardly believe that I was walking in such a high degree of the glory and presence of God. I was tasting a piece of heaven here on earth in Dallas, Texas under a star-colored night. One detail I do remember very clearly; an arc-shaped moon that seemed to be smiling down at me accentuated the night sky. God is always good, even in the little things.

THE VISION OF THE RIVER OF BLOOD

Little did I realize that what I would experience next would draw me deeper into the glory and presence of God. I must forewarn you, the vision that I am about to describe is hard to explain, especially since as I have shared with you earlier, I was lost in the glory. What I can tell you with absolute certainty is that Jesus showed me a prophetic vision that was so real and powerful, it has forever changed the course of my life and that of thousands others. It was as if I was inside the vision myself. Moreover, the vision answered the question,

"How can we overturn, reverse and destroy
the demonically engineered patterns of behavior in our lives
that keep us from living in victory?"

The vision began when **I could see several people standing in front of a stream of blood.** In my spirit, I knew instantly that the people I was seeing were followers of Jesus. Again, it was as if I was inside the vision and this became even more real to me when I heard the Lord Jesus utter the words, "Come closer."

As I approached the stream of blood, I began to hear strange and very distinct high frequency noises I can only describe as several broken radios that were broadcasting and mixing several different frequencies. The noise coming from the stream of blood was quite eerie! When I realized that the disturbing noise was coming directly from the stream of blood; I remember asking the question, "What is this noise Lord?" The Lord Jesus responded immediately in a manner that I will never ever forget. In fact, I can clearly remember that the response left me speechless.

THE SOUND OF INIQUITY

Jesus said to me, "This noise is the sound of the iniquities of the forefathers that Satan uses to harass or hinder my people's destiny." I was immediately reminded of the voice of righteous Able's blood that cried from the ground beneath for vengeance. Cain could not escape his punishment because the voice of his brother's blood appealed for justice from the throne of God. God was summoned to avenge Able's untimely death at the hands of his jealous brother.

God said to Cain, "Where is Abel your brother?" He said, "How should I know?
Am I his babysitter?" 10-12 God said, "What have you done! The voice of your
brother's blood is calling to me from the ground. From now on you'll get nothing but
curses from this ground; you'll be driven from this ground that has opened
its arms to receive the blood of your murdered brother. You'll farm this ground,
but it will no longer give you its best. You'll be a homeless wanderer on Earth." Genesis 4:9-12

The Lord Jesus continued instructing me, ***"Tell My people that I***
want to silence these voices of iniquity in their blood, if they are willing
to exchange their corrupted bloodlines for My uncorrupted bloodline."
Then, suddenly I saw the group of believers JUMP OVER the stream of
blood and when their feet landed on the other side of the stream, the Blood
river behind them disappeared instantly. If you are interested in seeing
what I saw, **please go to Youtube and type in "Genetic Salvation" in the**
search engine. The interview I had with my friend Sid Roth, host of "Its
Supernatural Television Show" will come up.

As soon as the blood disappeared, I saw the Spirit of God come upon
this group of believers and they started praising God with great intensity. I
remember asking, "What happened to the stream of blood?" Immediately,
Jesus answered me by saying, "I have cut if off their lives. It's gone. Satan
can no longer use it against them."

I was stunned and excited at the same time.

Just imagine having everything in your past that is holding you back from
moving forward and experiencing Heaven on Earth, including the past iniquities
of your forefathers, disappear in an instant. Imagine becoming "FREE" in an
instant from all of your negative genetic proclivities and in the process, ensuring
that Satan can no longer use your past to impend your future. Still caught up in
the vision, I can remember thinking, **"How is this even possible?"**

"Tell My people that I want to silence these voices of iniquity in their
blood if they are willing to exchange their corrupted bloodlines for My
uncorrupted bloodline."

JUMPING OVER THE STREAM OF BLOOD!

At that very moment, I heard the voice of the Lord again. He began to give
me another instruction. He said, **"Do to My people what I have shown you**
and you will see many miracles!" Then, the Lord Jesus proceeded to show

50

me "how" all believers can "JUMP" over their corrupted ancestral bloodline practically speaking. The process is really quite simple; it consists of two parts. The first part is a **powerful prayer of renunciation,** which is a prayer that formally and specifically allows you to renounce your spiritual and emotional allegiance to corrupted bloodline of your forefathers in order to appropriate the "incorruptible bloodline" of Jesus Christ. The second part of the act is a prophetic act of **"Jumping the Bloodline,"** by faith. This second part of the prophetic at is what has commonly become referred to as **JTL** or (Jumping the Line).

Jesus promised me that if anyone would **"Jump the Line,"** they would be able to have everything in their past that is holding them back from moving forward and experiencing Heaven on Earth, including the past iniquities of our forefathers, disappear in an instant. In the process, God would ensure that Satan could no longer use our past against us. I tucked away this promise in my heart. All of a sudden, I could see the stars and moon again in the Texas sky. My prophetic encounter and vision was over.

The next thing I can remember is that I found myself standing in front of the main entrance to the Gaylord Resort. It took me a moment to adjust to my surroundings and fully realize what had just happened. Once I had regained my composure, I realized where I was and remembered I had a meeting that I had to attend to.

When I greeted the businessmen I was scheduled to meet, I am sure they sensed something was a bit off and different about me, even though no one mentioned anything. I am so confident of this because all throughout the meeting, my spirit was literally jumping on the inside of me, trying to process everything that had just transpired. All the while trying to figure out what I was to do with what Jesus had just shared with me. I knew that there was no going back.

I can tell you, the meeting with my business friends could not have ended fast enough. As I am sure you can imagine, during the entire meeting, all I could think of was going somewhere that I could have peace and quiet, so I could figure all this out. However, that was not to be.

The truth of the matter is that even after the meeting was over and I did find a quiet place, it took me quite a while to figure it all out. For quite a while, I did not mention my encounter to my friends and those close to me who I really trust. And if the truth be told, I still have not figured out everything from my glorious encounter with the Lord. To this day, several years later, I am still receiving a deeper and more detailed revelation of my "Walk with Jesus" in Texas. However, there is one thing I have figured out for sure . . .

When you "Jump the Line," your life will be forever changed!!!

CHAPTER TEN

BEFORE YOU JUMP 1.0

*The LORD is the portion of my inheritance and my cup; You support my lot.
The lines have fallen to me in pleasant places; Indeed, my heritage is beautiful to me.
Psalm 16:5-6 (NKJV)*

ARE YOU READY TO JUMP THE LINE?

If you are ready to "Jump The Line," I am ready to lead you though the process of renouncing your spiritual umbilical cord to the corrupted bloodlines of your natural ancestors. This process involves "the prayer of renunciation and a powerful prophetic act called "Jumping The Line!" I am ready to pray with you right here and right now through this book. You can also find the prayer video for this prayer inside our one of a kind Mobile App that we developed called "Jump The Line". Go to www.ijumpedtheline.com or francismyles.com to download the App to your smart phone or tablet. You can also search for the App on the Apple or Google Play Store under the search parameters "Jump the line: Freedom."

However, before you even consider "Jumping The Line," there are a few things I want to address first. To begin with, I have several initial suggestions for you to consider before "Jumping The Line." As with anything of importance and significance in life, "Jumping The Line" should not be taken lightly - - - in this case, you should LITERALLY think through this before you take the leap of faith:

1. **If you are not ready, don't jump . . .better still wait.**
   "Jumping The Line" is not for the person who has accepted as normal their addictions or diseases. It is not for people who have created a community of comfort within their misery. "Jumping The Line" is for God-fearing believers in the body of Christ and anyone who is willing to draw a "line" against demonically engineered addictions, misfortunes and genetic anomalies. **"Jumping The Line" is for people who are ready to change their now…."Now!"**

2. **Don't get over emotional.**
   Emotion will most likely accompany the process of "Jumping The Line," but not always. My suggestion is not to get overly excited and emotional as you "Jump The Line." Do not place demands on "Jumping The Line" that are unrealistic. Remember, you may experience something spectacular or you may not. Regardless, you will experience something supernatural. However many people really become emotional after they "Jump The Line" and suddenly realize that they are finally, **"Free at last!"**

3. **Jumping the Line is between you and God.**
   You do not need to share what you are doing with everyone in advance. And you do not need to report every detail of the process, as you are going through it, with your social networks. Jumping the line is not a process that is focused on getting public attention. Rather, "Jumping The Line" is a very personal and intimate prophetic act that allows you to walk in the freedom you were destined for. But feel FREE to share this book and our JTL Mobile App using the "Share Button" inside the App with your friends and family.

4. **Faith helps** – I have seen miracles for people who "Jumped The Line" without knowing fully what they were doing. So it is clear that God does and moves as he pleases. Still, we do know that everything connected to God and his Son Jesus Christ is based on faith. Many times in the Gospels the Lord Jesus told many of those He healed, "Go for your faith has made you whole." This expression means that faith is an important tool to experiencing miracles. In Hebrews 11:6 the Bible says that "without faith it is impossible to please God."

5. **Forgiveness opens up possibilities** – Before you "Jump The Line" I would suggest taking a moment to open your heart to God and see if there is anyone you have yet to forgive or anyone who you hold resentment towards. I suggest this because very often I have seen unforgiveness hold someone back from experiencing the blessings God wants to pour out on them. If you feel forgiveness is just too much for you to bear, then I would say that might be **one of the sidelines** you may want to consider Jumping first.

6. **Jumping The Line is the beginning of your "Total Transformation"**
   – "Jumping The Line" is not a magic wand but it is very powerful and scriptural. However after you "Jump The Line" you must take responsibility for maintaining your newfound freedom in Christ – it's so easy to go back to the other side of the bloodline if you are not careful and allow the devil to trick you. Give no room to the devil after Christ sets you "Free!"

JUMP the LINE

CHAPTER ELEVEN

BEFORE YOU JUMP 2.0

The very credentials these people are waving around as something special, I'm tearing up and throwing out with the trash—along with everything else I used to take credit for. And why? Because of Christ. Yes, all the things I once thought were so important are gone from my life. Compared to the high privilege of knowing Christ Jesus as my Master, firsthand, everything I once thought I had going for me is insignificant—dog dung. I've dumped it all in the trash so that I could embrace Christ and be embraced by him. Philippians 3:7-9

Moving forward, before you "Jump The Line," there are a few basic instructions I need to cover with you.

1. Before we pray, I need all men and single women to remember two (2) names: your **Fathers last name** and your **mother's maiden name**. But for all married and divorced women I want you to remember three (3) names, **Your Fathers last name, your mother's maiden name and your husband or ex-husbands last name.**

We are going to use these Surnames to identify the appropriate bloodlines and lineages that we are going to renounce legally before the Courts of Heaven so the devil has no legal grounds to visit us with generational iniquities or curses. It is important for you to remember that I am not asking you to renounce your father, mother or husband. I am only using their surnames to legally identify the corrupted bloodlines or lineages of their ancestors.

In the book of Philippians chapter three, the Apostle Paul tells us how he counted as loss his natural bloodline or lineage in order to possess the priceless knowledge of the Lord Jesus Christ. He came to realize that his natural pedigree as a member of the Tribe of Benjamin was like cow-dung compared to what God offers us in Christ.

Please remember that the **New Covenant** is a Covenant of **Appropriation** and **Divine Exchange.** When we come to the foot of the Cross we exchange our Sin for His righteousness; our sicknesses for His healing; our mind for the Mind of Christ. So it follows that we have to exchange our **"Corrupted Bloodlines for the Messiah's Incorruptible Bloodline?"** Doesn't it?

Once again I am NOT asking you to renounce your "Father, Mother or Husband." The LORD instructed me to tell people who are seeking deliverance from generational curses to renounce their spiritual allegiances to their corrupted bloodlines and exchange them for a "new allegiance" to the Uncorrupted bloodline of the LORD Jesus Christ.

2. When we start praying, I want you to add the WORD **"Bloodline or Lineage"** to the Surname of your Father, Mother and Husband, when you start renouncing your spiritual allegiance to these corrupted ancestral bloodlines.

For example if your father's last name is Jackson…You will say "Jackson Lineage or Bloodline" not just "Jackson" during the prayer of renunciation. If your mother's maiden name is "Lopez"…You will say "Lopez Lineage or Bloodline." Once again you are NOT renouncing your Father, Mother or Husband, you are simply **cutting the spiritual umbilical cord** between yourself and these "sin corrupted or ravaged bloodlines" that originate from the first Adam.

3. Please get a "Red Ribbon" or anything that represents a "Line" and place it on the floor in front of your feet. This "Line" on the floor will represent the bloodlines or ancestral lines that you need to "Jump over" to experience the freedom you seek.

Why do I have to renounce my spiritual allegiance to my natural bloodline or lineage?

The answer is very simple but deeply profound. **What you fail to renounce remains attached to you.** When the Lord Jesus Christ gave me the revelation on "Jumping The Line," He told me that His people would never experience total freedom from generational curses and genetic anomaly if they are still holding on to the **"ration or portion of Genes"** that they inherited from their natural ancestors. Just like no man can serve two masters. We cannot serve two bloodlines (our ancestral bloodline and the Messiah's bloodline). We have to choose between the two.

The Lord told me that just as we exchanged our sins for His righteousness, we must also exchange our old corrupted bloodlines for His flawless bloodline. This is the trajectory of the glorious divine exchange. If we do not legally renounce or cut our spiritual umbilical cord with our corrupted lineage the devil has every legal right to use iniquities attached to our bloodline against us.

If I renounce my bloodline, will I also be renouncing my godly heritage?

The answer is a resounding NO! I also asked the Holy Spirit about this when the Lord gave me this revelation. Here is what the Holy Spirit told me. He told me that **every good and perfect gift comes from the LORD and none of us is good except God.** He told me that every thing that is good about any of our natural ancestors is simply an extension of the vast goodness of God. So when we renounce our spiritual allegiance to our ancestor's corrupted bloodlines or lineages we are only denouncing everything else that is attached to our bloodline that is not of God.

JUMP the LINE

JUMP the LINE

CHAPTER TWELVE
JUMPING THE LINE PRAYER

When Solomon finished praying, a bolt of lightning out of heaven struck the
Whole-Burnt-Offering and sacrifices and the Glory of God filled The Temple.
The Glory was so dense that the priests couldn't get in—God so filled The Temple
that there was no room for the priests! When all Israel saw the fire fall from heaven and
the Glory of God fill The Temple, they fell on their knees, bowed their heads,
and worshiped, thanking God: Yes! God is good! His love never quits! 2 Chronicles 7:1-3

Can you feel the pulsating of the Power of the Holy Spirit all around you right now? I am so excited for you. But before you jump over the "prophetic bloodline" do not forget to give Jesus your highest praise once you jump over the prophetic bloodline. The Psalmist tells us that we are to come through His gates with thanksgiving but when we are in His court; we are to give Him our highest praise. Praise is the spiritual protocol of entering the courts of Heaven.

Praise Him for your deliverance, praise Him for healing you, and praise Him for clarity of mind, peace and joy. Praise Him for breaking generational curses. Are you ready to JUMP the LINE? I want you to JUMP over the Line the moment I tell you to.

JUMP THE LINE PRAYER INTRO:

The prayer that you are about to go through is the prayer that the Holy Spirit gave me for taking any person through complete deliverance, from all **"Generational curses, recurring behavior patterns, addictions and genetic anomalies."** Please feel free to read it aloud before you JUMP the LINE. You have to pray the prayer loudly. Praying the prayer out aloud will release both your faith and the awesome power of God.

JUMP THE LINE PRAYER:

(Please repeat after ME)

"Heavenly Father, I stand in your royal courtroom to receive your righteous judgment over my bloodline inheritance. Heavenly Father I call upon your holy angels to be enforcers and witnesses to this legal and righteous transaction. I also decree and declare that all the demonic powers that have ever been attached to the bloodlines of my natural ancestors will respect and honor your righteous judgment over my genetic inheritance.

Heavenly Father your Word says that if we confess our sins, you are faithful and just to forgive our sin and cleanse us from all unrighteousness. Heavenly Father forgive me for worshiping or idolizing my family ancestry instead of giving it up for the sake of Christ my Lord (Phil 3:5-8). Heavenly Father I choose to forgive every person who has ever hurt me even as you forgave me in Christ Jesus. I let go of every root of bitterness in Jesus name.

1# DENOUNCING YOUR NATURAL FATHER'S CORRUPTED LINEAGE

Heavenly Father, I willingly and joyfully DENOUNCE.....(Insert YOUR father's last name here with the word LINEAGE or BLOODLINE attached to it)!

I denounce the bloodline and lineage that this name represents and all the demonic technologies, proclivities and iniquities that are attached to it throughout the timeline of this bloodline can no longer influence my life and destiny. I give up this bloodline to possess Yeshua's holy and flawless prophetic bloodline and lineage. I decree and declare that Jesus' genetic inheritance is now my inheritance.

2# DENOUNCING YOUR NATURAL MOTHER'S CORRUPTED LINEAGE

Heavenly Father, I willingly and joyfully DENOUNCE.....(Insert YOUR mother's maiden name here with the word LINEAGE or BLOODLINE attached to it)!

I denounce the bloodline and lineage that this name represents and all the demonic technologies, proclivities and iniquities that are attached to it throughout the timeline of this lineage can no longer influence my life. I give up this bloodline to possess Yeshua's holy and flawless prophetic bloodline and lineage. I decree and declare that Jesus' genetic inheritance is now my inheritance.

3# DENOUNCING YOUR NATURAL HUSBAND'S CORRUPTED LINEAGE

Heavenly Father, I willingly and joyfully DENOUNCE.....(Married and divorced women Insert YOUR husband's last name here with the word LINEAGE or BLOODLINE attached to it)!

I denounce the bloodline and lineage that this name represents and all the demonic technologies, proclivities and iniquities that are attached to it throughout the timeline of this bloodline can no longer influence my life and destiny. I give up this bloodline to possess Yeshua's holy and flawless prophetic bloodline and lineage. I decree and declare that Jesus' genetic inheritance is now my inheritance.

4# (FOR PEOPLE WHO NEVER KNEW THEIR BIOLOGICAL PARENTS) DENOUNCING YOUR NATURAL PARENT'S CORRUPTED LINEAGE

Heavenly Father, I do not know my biological parents but you do. I willingly and joyfully DENOUNCE…the corrupted genetics of my natural parents lineage!

I denounce the lineages or bloodlines that their names represent and all the demonic technologies, proclivities and iniquities that are attached to their bloodlines throughout the timeline of these lineages can no longer influence my life. I give up these lineages to possess Yeshua's holy and flawless prophetic bloodline and lineage. I decree and declare that Jesus' genetic inheritance is now my inheritance.

5# DENOUNCING ALL DEMONICALLY SUPERIMPOSED DNA

Heavenly Father, I willingly and joyfully DENOUNCE.....
all SUPERIMPOSED DNA, arising from Witchcraft, Sexual Assault, Blood
Transfusions, Trauma, Sexual Immorality, Adoption, Rejection or Mind
Control. I strongly DENOUNCE all the demonic technologies, proclivities
and iniquities that are attached to this Superimposed DNA throughout the
timeline of its lineage. I give it up to possess Yeshua's holy and flawless
prophetic DNA. I decree that this demonically engineered Superimposed
DNA can no longer influence my life and destiny.

6# DENOUNCING ALL TRAUMATIC MEMORIES AND TRIGGERING MECHANISMS ATTACHED TO YOUR OLD DNA

Heavenly Father, I willingly and joyfully DENOUNCE.....all Traumatic
memories and emotional triggering mechanisms in my brain that was attached
to the bloodlines and Superimposed DNA that I have henceforth renounced
before this Supreme and Royal Court. I petition you Heavenly Father to issue
a decree immediately releasing me from all of these traumatic memories and
emotional triggering mechanisms in the name of the Lord Jesus Christ.

7# DENOUNCING ALL ILLEGAL TRADES MADE BY SELF AND FOREFATHERS ON SATAN'S TRADING FLOORS

Heavenly Father, as I prepare to jump over the prophetic bloodline, I
denounce all Illegals trades that I and my forefathers have ever made on
Satan's trading floors that have given Satan the legal grounds to create havoc
in my bloodline. I repent in Yeshua's name for all violations against God's
Law and Holiness that my ancestors and me created on Satan's trading
floors. Heavenly Father I petition your Royal and Supreme Court to issue
a decree releasing me from all the spiritual consequences of these illegal
trades. I decree and declare that when I jump over the prophetic bloodline
Satan will lose all legal grounds to access my NEW DNA in Yeshua's name

Heavenly Father, as I prepare to jump over the prophetic bloodline, I
release my faith for the healing of my body and all genetic anomalies in
Yeshua's name I pray. Heavenly Father, I also beseech you to deliver me
permanently from all generational curses in my bloodline, by superimposing
Yeshua's flawless prophetic bloodline over me. Thank you for healing me
from any and all genetic deficiencies, in the name of Jesus Christ. I also

decree that when I jump over the prophetic bloodline I will be jumping directly into the glory realm of God where all miracles reside in Yeshua's name I pray. Amen

JUMPING OVER THE LINE:

Enter His gates with thanksgiving And His courts with praise.

Give thanks to Him, bless His name. Psalm 100:4 (NKJV)

Before you Jump over the "prophetic bloodline" do not forget to give Yeshua (Jesus) your highest praise after you jump over the line. The bible admonishes us to come through His gates with thanksgiving but the protocol of entering the "Courts of Heaven" is "PRAISE!" So after you "Jump The Line" you must go into serious praise before God. Its after people "Jump The Line" that they start experiencing the miracles of "Jumping The Line." Are you READY to "Jump the Line" now? Here we go, "In the name of the Father, the Son and the Holy Spirit I say JUMP OVER THE LINE in Yeshua's might name!!! Hallelujah LORD, thank you for delivering your people from every generational curse, every witchcraft curse, addictions, failures, misfortunes and all genetic anomalies in the name of Jesus Christ of Nazareth." Amen

JUMP the  LINE

CHAPTER THIRTEEN

SHARE!

As Jesus was getting into the boat, the demon-delivered man begged to go along, but he wouldn't let him. Jesus said, "Go home to your own people. Tell them your story—what the Master did, how he had mercy on you." The man went back and began to preach in the Ten Towns area about what Jesus had done for him. He was the talk of the town. Mark 5:18-20

Now that you have jumped the line and you realize just how transformative the experience truly is you can imagine the calls, the cries for help, the desperate needs that come to us, as a ministry that impacting people internationally. Some of the people in desperate need of help do not have smart phones to download our "Jump The Line" mobile app to. To reach this people we need you to become our voice and feet. Our focus is to help millions of people, "Jump the line" and find true freedom that has eluded many of them, including many Christians. Every person is precious to God; therefore they are precious to us. *Your partnership in actively telling people about this book or sharing our JTL Mobile App puts you right in the middle of this incredible work that God is doing!!!*

EVERYTHING COUNTS!

Whatever the LORD moves on your heart to contribute to become a World Changer will be greatly appreciated. We are truly excited that thousands of people from around the world are experiencing miracles ever since they "Jumped The Line." I am so thankful to my friend Sid Roth host of "Its Supernatural" whose Television ministry helped me take the revelation of "Jumping the line" to thousands of people around the world We also want to translate the contents of this book and our Mobile App into other languages to reach more people with this powerful message of FREEDOM. Please pray about sowing into this wonderful project.

Please JOIN our freedom campaign and help us take 1 million people through the act of Jumping of the line! Our main goal is to have 100 Million people jump the line before the year 2022. **You can elect to contribute as little as $5 dollars or as much as $10,000 to help us reach our target. You donations will go to purchasing more copies of this book that will be given away to people who cant afford this book. Just make sure that your check memo says "Project Jump The Line."** Remember the Bible says that it is more blessed to give than to receive. **Please share this book or Mobile App with 10 friends on Facebook or with family members.** Please visit the App Store or go to www.ijumpedtheline.com to download our one-of-a-kind "Jump the line" mobile app. Order more copies of this book to giveaway to friends at www.francismyles.com or on Amazon For special bulk order discounts please call our ministry office (602-888-0364) or email us at info@francismyles.com.

JUMP the LINE

CHAPTER FOURTEEN
NOW WHAT?

Hearing that, they walked away, one after another, beginning with the oldest.
The woman was left alone. Jesus stood up and spoke to her. "Woman, where are they?
Does no one condemn you?" 11 "No one, Master." "Neither do I," said Jesus.
"Go on your way. From now on, don't sin." John 8:9-11

Jumping the line is not the end of mastering true freedom, rather the beginning of it. Now that you have jumped the line, the challenge you will face is STAYING over the "Line." Yes, the cross comes with power and authority and, because you have made the CHOICE to Jump the Line, you have said with faith that the **past has no more power over you.**

However, this does not mean that Satan will not try to tempt you. But just remember what we said earlier, that temptation is a choice. You have a CHOICE to stay over the line or go back to the unrestored side of the bloodline. The truth is, Satan will come against you and try to tell you nothing has happened to you or that "Jumping The Line" will not work for you. I tell you this not to scare you, but to prepare you. But greater is He who is in you than he (the devil) who is in the world.

My dear children, you come from God and belong to God. You have already
won a big victory over those false teachers, for the Spirit in you is far
stronger than anything in the world. 1 John 4:4

REMEMBER THIS
Satan wants to keep you on the unrestored side of the bloodline!

ALSO REMEMBER THIS
Satan has no authority over your life, unless you give it to him. Jesus said' "it is finished", so that settles it!

SO what do you do? What can you do practically to resist the enemy and stay over the line? The following are a few actions you can take to stay on the restored side of the bloodline.

1. **Learn as much as you can about your father God, your heavenly family and your true identity in Christ** – Specifically, I am suggesting you read your bible regularly. The more you learn about God, Jesus, the Kingdom of God and who you are as a believer, the easier it is to resist thoughts of doubt and unbelief from the enemy.

2. **Talk to your Heavenly Father** – Regularly; I am referring to spending time with God in prayer. Remember prayer is not a ritual, rather the opportunity to openly talk with God.

3. **Don't neglect the importance of fellowship and community** – Become involved in regular fellowship with other like-minded people, especially those who have jumped the line. Find a bible based life-giving church near you and if that does not fill you up we will have lots of powerful services online if you join our online community. All our Sunday services are streamed live at www.royalpriesthoodembassy.com

4. **Upgrade your relationships** – Remember when the wrong people exit your life the wrong things stop happening to you. When the right people enter your life good things begin happening to you. Its time for you to get some God-fearing friends.

5. **Upgrade your environment** – Change your environment. Do not keep an environment around you that could reinforce the past that God has delivered you from. (For instance alcoholics should never hang out in bars. It's a bad combination.)

6. **Tap into the wisdom of others** – There is nothing or nobody you can learn from better than the Bible. However this does not mean there are not other resources available to you such as, books, video, podcasts, plus a host of other avenues for renewing your mind and growing your spirit.

7. **Declare it!** – Make spontaneous but heartfelt declarations about your newfound freedom and the life you desire to live. (Write them down in your journal).

8. **Be thankful** – Jumping The Line is a precious gift from God, don't take it for granted

9. **Share your experience with others**– One of the best ways to maintain and explode your "Freedom" is to share it with others. This keeps you accountable to the process of staying free after "Jumping The Line." Please click on the "Share ICON" inside our "Jump the Line" Mobile App and share the App with your friends and family. Buy several copies of this book for your family, friends and co-workers as birthday, anniversary or Christmas presents.

JUMP the LINE

CHAPTER FIFTEEN
DEALING WITH SIDELINES

In chapter two I promised that I would take you deeper into understanding "Sidelines" and how to deal with them. I have already made it clear that life is full of defining lines, but the most important lines are "Bloodlines and Sidelines." Bloodlines are genetic and generational whereas "Sidelines" are immediate and situational. But some sidelines can have a paralyzing effect on actualizing destiny and manifesting a person's full potential. While I was growing up in Africa, I had a chance to play soccer with some boys will dazzling football skills. Many of them came from poor families. I was sure they would all have successful football careers. But I was grossly mistaken. Despite their dazzling football skills, many of them were sidelined from going any further by crippling personal insecurity and scandalous behavior off the field. A part of me wished I could wave a magic wand and move them past their spiritual, mental or emotional sidelines because I was such a fan of their dazzling football skills. Now, I know that **"you can never succeed for someone else or wishful think them into becoming what they are not internally!"**

SIDELINES THAT CAN LEAD TO MURDER

Time passed. Cain brought an offering to GOD from the produce of his farm. Abel also brought an offering, but from the firstborn animals of his herd, choice cuts of meat. GOD liked Abel and his offering, but Cain and his offering didn't get his approval. Cain lost his temper and went into a sulk.[6-7] GOD spoke to Cain: "Why this tantrum? Why the sulking? If you do well, won't you be accepted? And if you don't do well, sin is lying in wait for you, ready to pounce; it's out to get you, you've got to master it."[8] Cain had words with

73

his brother. They were out in the field; Cain came at Abel his brother and killed him.
Genesis 4:3-8

The above biblical story illustrates how dangerous some sidelines car become. In this case Cain's sidelines led him to murder his innocent brother in a jealousy rage directed at God. The sidelines that Cain failed to conquer and jump over were "Pride, Rejection and Unforgiveness." Cain and his brother both approached the presence of God with an offering. Apparently Adam and Eve had already told their two sons that God only accepts "blood sacrifices" to effect atonement for Sin. When Adam and Eve sinned against God in the Garden of Eden, the Lord killed an innocent animal and clothed them with its blood (Genesis 3:21), that's when they realized that without the shedding of blood there is no remission of sins (Hebrews 9:27).

Its clear from following this story to its logical conclusion that they were three main sidelines that he failed to conquer or jump over than ultimately did him in. The first sideline was obviously "Pride." It is only pride that can make a man approach a God who requires a "blood sacrifice" with a sacrifice of "vegetables." Even though growing vegetables was Cain's main profession he could have easily traded his vegetables for a sheep or goat from his brother's farm. But the pride in his heart sidelined him from doing the right thing. Consequently, God rejected Cain's offering of vegetables and accepted his young brother's blood sacrifice.

God's rejection of Cain's offering immediately opened him up to another equally powerful sideline "Rejection!" How many people do you know of who have been sidelined for years by the spirit of rejection. It colors and filters its way into everything they do. Thousands of viable marital and business relationships have been sacrificed at the altars of rejection. Its time for you to "Jump over" this crippling sideline, by first realizing that Jesus Christ took ALL of your rejection on the Cross. Listen to this…

There was nothing attractive about him, nothing to cause us to take a second look.
He was looked down on and passed over, a man who suffered, who knew pain firsthand.
One look at him and people turned away. We looked down on him, thought he was scum.
But the fact is, it was our pains he carried—our disfigurements, all the things wrong with us.
We thought he brought it on himself, that God was punishing him for his own failures.
But it was our sins that did that to him, that ripped and tore and crushed him—our sins!
He took the punishment, and that made us whole. Isaiah 53:3-6

Cain felt so rejected by God that in a classical case of "misplace anger" he developed deep dislike for his brother as though his brother had any control on God. God seeing the absurdity of Cain's rage, warned him against the "Sin" that was crouching like a tiger at the door of his heart. God told him that if he did the right thing (bringing a blood sacrifice) God would also show him His favor. Sound simple ha? But to a man with a heart infested with both pride and rejection…simple…is never simple! Instead Cain drove through the "red light" of God's fatherly warning and deceived his trusting brother to join him for a field walk. While walking in the woods, Cain pounced upon his unsuspecting brother and killed him. Suddenly Cain became the willing prisoner of another insidious sideline "Murder!"

As the blood of innocent Able spilled into the ground below, its voice reached the ears of God. God's judgment concerning the spilling of the blood of innocent Able was both swift and severe. He banished Cain from His presence forever, in this life and the after life! Wow, what a tragic sentence! Somebody said that the greatest punishment in hell is not the fiery flames but the knowledge that a person has been banished from the presence of God forever. What I really want you to take note of is that the "lines" that destroyed Cain were not bloodlines, but situations (Sidelines) he failed to master.

What "Sidelines" are you Wrestling with, Now?

In our one-of-a-kind "Jump The Line" Mobile App we have a section within the App that deals with the different "Sidelines" that we all deal with on a daily basis. The App also includes very powerful prayers of how to diffuse and jump over the sidelines that are hindering you from going FORWARD in God. I have included a sample teaching on a Sideline taught in the Mobile App and the prayer that goes with it. But to get all my teachings and prayers on "Sidelines" please download the "Jump The Line" mobile App @ ijumpedtheline.com or in the Apple Store or Google Play Store.

DEALING WITH WITCHCRAFT SIDELINE

Having been born in Africa, I know firsthand the reality of Witchcraft. My first encounter with supernatural power was with witches and wizards. These men and women were very well versed in their chosen profession. When night fell upon our township, great fear would come upon us all, because we knew that the witches worked best in the night hours. We would hear strange eerie sounds and footsteps of invisible beings jumping from roof to roof. Our spiritual senses were heightened by the nightly activity of these forces of evil. But witchcraft and the belief in the occult are not restricted to Africa; this demonic profession is a global phenomenon. Most importantly these evil practices are as old as the fall of man in the Garden of Eden.

God warned the children of Israel (Deuteronomy 18:9-14) against being involved in this practice, because practicing witchcraft in any form always attracts the judgment of God and curses that travel through several generations. Some of the most powerful generational curses, I have encountered since the Lord Jesus called me to the ministry of deliverance are usually connected to pervasive involvement in witchcraft by the person seeking deliverance or their natural ancestors. But contending with the spirit of witchcraft is not always generational; in many instances it is "situational!" When witchcraft is "situational" it has the power to sideline people from living in the true freedom that Christ offers in His Word.

If you or members of your family have ever been involved in the "Occult," especially in practicing Witchcraft, you may be dealing with witchcraft curses attached to your ancestral bloodline. You may consider repenting on behalf of your ancestors for these acts of evil against God and other people. This is referred to as "identification repentance." The prophet Daniel gives us the best example of the power of identification repentance when he repented before God on behalf of the nation of Israel (Daniel 9:4-10).

OTHER FORMS OF WITCHCRAFT

Additionally, there are two other forms of witchcraft other than the "professional witchcraft" that we have described above. These two forms are subtler than the first, so they are not so easy to detect. But the Bible shows us that God hates these two forms of witchcraft just as much as He hates the first. I will quickly list these two other forms:

1. Witchcraft which is moving from the Spirit to the flesh

O foolish Galatians! Who has bewitched you that you should not obey the truth, before whose eyes Jesus Christ was clearly portrayed among you as crucified? ² This only I want to learn from you: Did you receive the Spirit by the works of the law, or by the hearing of faith? ³ Are you so foolish? Having begun in the Spirit, are you now being made perfect by the flesh? (Galatians 3:1-3 NKJV).

In the book of Galatians, the Apostle Paul informs followers of Christ at the church of Galatia that they were under a spell of witchcraft. He informs

76

them of this by posing the question, "Who has bewitched you?" The witchcraft in this passage has to do with them beginning to do through the arm of the flesh what they started doing in the Spirit. How many times do we all confront this "Sideline" between walking in the Spirit and walking in the flesh? This book and our mobile app is about "jumping lines." We have loaded them with tools on how to walk in the Spirit and break the power of the arm of the flesh over your life.

2. Witchcraft which is rebellion against God's authority

"But I did obey the Lord," Saul insisted. "I carried out the mission he gave me. I brought back King Agag, but I destroyed everyone else. [21] Then my troops brought in the best of the sheep, goats, cattle, and plunder to sacrifice to the Lord your God in Gilgal." [22] But Samuel replied, "What is more pleasing to the Lord: your burnt offerings and sacrifices or your obedience to his voice? Listen! Obedience is better than sacrifice, and submission is better than offering the fat of rams. [23] Rebellion is as sinful as witchcraft, and stubbornness as bad as worshiping idols. So because you have rejected the command of the Lord, he has rejected you as king" (1 Samuel 15:20-23 NLT).

Finally, there is another form of witchcraft that God truly hates. It is the witchcraft, which is rebellion against God's authority. **The Scriptures declare that stubbornness or rebellion is like practicing witchcraft**. What is interesting is that years after the prophet Samuel gave this admonition to King Saul, the rebellious king continued rebelling against God's authority and actually ended consulting with mediums (witches) for spiritual direction. Some of you reading this passage need to "jump the line" between "stubbornness" and "total obedience to God." You need to start living on the redeemed side of the "line" where stubbornness comes to an end and you start enjoying the blessings that follow a life lived in obedience to God.

JUMPING OVER WITCHCRAFT SIDELINE PRAYER:

The prayer that you are about to go through is the prayer that the Holy Spirit gave me for taking any person through complete deliverance, from any "Spirit of Witchcraft" that has sidelined you from experiencing the victorious life that Christ purchased for you on the Cross. Please feel free to read it aloud or download the AUDIO prayer inside our "Jump The Line" Mobile App and repeat after me before you JUMP the LINE. You have to pray the prayer loudly.

JUMP the LINE

(Please read loudly)

"Heavenly Father, I stand in your royal courtroom to receive your righteous judgment against the spirit of Witchcraft that is working against me Heavenly Father I call upon your holy angels to be enforcers and witnesses to this legal and righteous transaction. I also decree and declare that al the demonic powers who are behind the spirit of witchcraft that has been sidelining me from experiencing what Jesus Christ purchased for me with His blood will respect and honor your righteous judgment that nothing shal by any means hurt me. I decree and enforce my position of victory agains the sideline of witchcraft. It is written... *"There is no divination agains. Jacob, no evil omens against Israel. It will now be said of Jacob and o, Israel, 'See what God has done!"* Numbers 23:23*

Heavenly Father, I decree and declare that I am the Jacob and Israel of God therefore there is no witchcraft, divination, incantations, spells, hexes or evi omens that can work against me, in the name of Jesus. It is written...*No weapor forged against you will prevail, and you will refute every tongue that accuse. you. This is the heritage of the servants of the Lord, and this is their vindicatior from me," declares the Lord. Isaiah 54:17*

Heavenly Father your Word says that if we confess our sins, you are faithfu and just to forgive our sin and cleanse us from all unrighteousness. Heavenly Father forgive me for anything that I did that opened the door for the spirit o: witchcraft to work against or through me. Heavenly Father I choose to forgive every person who has ever hurt me even as you forgave me in Christ Jesus. I le go of every root of bitterness in Jesus name. Heavenly Father as I NOW prepare to Jump over the Sideline of Witchcraft; I decree and declare that the BLOOD of JESUS will become a WALL of SEPARATION between me and the spirit o: witchcraft that has been harassing me, spiritually, emotionally and financially Witchcraft will no longer impact anything associated with me negatively, ir Jesus name, I pray.

JUMPING OVER THE SIDELINE OF WITCHCRAFT

(Before you Jump over this "Sideline" do not forget to give Yeshua you highest praise after you jump over the line.) HERE WE GO!!! In the name of the Father, the Son and the Holy Spirit JUMP and receive you FREEDOM!!! Amen."

JUMP the LINE

CHAPTER SIXTEEN

JOIN THE MOVEMENT!

The Lord gave the word; Great was the company of those who proclaimed it:
Psalm 68:11 (NKJV)

Thank you so much for the privilege of allowing me to JOIN you on your Journey to CHANGING YOUR NOW. Now that you have JUMPED the LINE your life will never ever be the same again. I know this for a fact. You have just changed your NOW! The fruit and after-effects of your deliverance will start manifesting all around you. Journal what starts happening in your life from this moment onwards.

Please share your glorious testimony with us at www.francismyles.com and JOIN thousands around the world who have also EXPERIENCED TOTAL FREEDOM after Jumping the Line! Please tell 10 friends or family members to get the "Jump the Line Mobile APP" on their cellphone or tablet by going to our website or inside the App Store or Google Play.

I have so much that I want to share with you. "Jumping over the LINE" is a major step towards transforming the quality of your life but it is just the beginning to stewarding the amazing miracles that are part of the aftermath. I have a 52 week mentoring program on 52 "Jump the Line Concepts" that will radically change your station in life and help you realize your highest dreams in a very short time. Please pray about joining my very exclusive "OVER-THE-LINE-COACHING PROGRAM" for a meager $199 per year. We will bring you cutting edge monthly mentorship, through Cutting edge

Videos, Weekly MP3 messages, Webinars, Conference calls and First Class
Articles. Join our very robust online social community of other likeminded
thinkers, movers and shakers. In addition as a member of my OVER-THE-
LINE Team you will get a "Diploma of Freedom Certificate" that you can
hang in your house as a memorial of the day you entered into the domain of
TOTAL FREEDOM after you "Jumped the Line." Please take time to visit
our "Web Store" @ francismyles.com for life transforming materials that
we have made available to you. Two of my bestselling books "The Order
of Melchizedek and The Consciousness of NOW" are amazing products to
start with. These book books will radically transform your life.